The Oz Affiliate's Guide to

CREATING YOUR OWN NICHE AFFILIATE WEBSITE

Matty Mac

Create your own Niche Affiliate Website

Before we start: Set up a G-mail account!
This will become very apparent as we go along, but you WILL need one.

Get a PAYPAL account. You WILL need one.

STEP 1 Find an affiliate product to sell

Checklist points:
- Find a product
- Competition Check
- Keyword search

First thing you need to do is FIND A PRODUCT to sell.

You can do this one of 2 ways. Buy a whole bunch of product, have it delivered to you, and then sell it on your site and send it out to customers.

OR find a product and become an AFFILIATE. The latter is what we are going to look at today. At a later date we will look at *Setting up a Shopify Website and selling your own product*.

NOW…This product really needs to be something that fits into your lifestyle. You need to be passionate about it.

It's far easier to sell something your passionate about, and you can mention in your everyday posts and discussions without it sounding "Sales-y".

If you really can't find a product to sell, check out my list of affiliate programs https://ozmattymac.com/affiliate-products-to-sell

When you THINK you have a product, head on over to google.

It's time to run a "Competition Check"
Pretend you were a customer looking for a product similar to yours..

Remember to search for the "Sizzle" not the "Steak", meaning...

If your product happened to be ***Big Bobs Hair Regeneration Lotion*** - Don't search the product. Search for "hair regenerating lotion" and similar. These are the KEYWORDS we are going to try to rank for.

What you should have before you is a whole list of products available, and what OUR aim is, is to appear on THIS page... somewhere.

Now, it's not the be-all, and end-all, if we don't, there are still a whole bunch of things we can do to drive traffic to our future site. BUT... if you do ever manage to crack this first page, you're on easy street!

NOW – Ask yourself, looking at this page...
CAN YOU SELL THIS PRODUCT BETTER THAN THESE GUYS?

Do you immediately think of new ideas, better text, a better video you could make, more WOW factor than that page…??

You need to OUT-DO these people, and In most cases, it's very possible to do so. If you have a little faith in yourself then back yourself! Go for it! Let's tackle it.

If what you're looking at is a very saturated market, like "Make Money online", then forget it. Start out with something a little easier to tackle, and as we go on you can conquer the world another time!

Let's do keyword search. Head on over to Google ADwords. Go into the Tools/Find Keywords section. Search for your related keyword. i.e.: Hair Regeneration

https://adwords.google.com/select/KeywordToolExternal

What you see is a list of ranking keywords. This is what the world is searching for, and what it gives you is a WHOLE BUNCH of NEW IDEAS!

Write down ALL of those keywords in this format:
{<= (Start with an open spintext bracket)
{hair growth|<= (Add a word break)
{hairgrowth|hairloss|hair loss cure|hair regrowth}<= (when you have listed them all, finish with a closed spintext bracket)

These are what is know as "Short Tail Keywords" 1 - 3 words.

{hair loss treatment for men|help me grow more hair} - These are known as "Long Tail Keywords"3 + words in a row.

So your list will look something like this.

{hair regeneration | hairgrowth | hairloss | hair loss cure | hairregrowth | hairtransplant | alopecia | hair loss treatment | hair growth products | hair transplant cost | hairfall | hairthinning | thinninghair | hairrestoration | hair loss treatment for men | hair loss in women | thinning hair women | alopeciatreatment | hair fall solution | baldnesscure | hair growth treatment | hair loss women | hairreplacement | hair loss causes | natural hair growth | hairimplants | hair loss prevention | hairtreatment | hair regrowth treatment | fast hair growth}

You can take this as far as you like..but pick about 20 relevant keywords. Next to these words in google you will see how many times in the month it has been searched.

Any keywords less than 500 really isn't worth ranking for, and any over 100,000 is probably going to be out of our price range, so stick to the in-betweeners!

So now you have a good basis to start with. Can you confidently check off the list?

- Find a product
- Competition Check
- Keyword search

Let's move on.

If you can't confidently move on, then maybe look for a new product, repeat and then move on.

STEP 2   Grab a great domain name

Head on over to a domain name site like GoDaddy.com and search – set up an account Try and use your keywords within your domain name.

You will have to think a little outside the box on this one. For example, if you tried to pick the domain www.curehairloss.com it has been taken, so be creative! I would probably be thinking something like:

curehairlosstoday.com
savemyhair.com
hairlosssavior.com

Grab a list of 5 or so available domain names and list them.

Think about what you have and choose something catchy, easy to remember, easy to market!

BUY THE DOMAIN!!

(**NOTE - Try to avoid using **hyphens** and stick to a **.com** suffix ** ie www.hair-save.info) Where the hell are you going to host this site? Great question. If you want a really quick, easy and cheap solution, head over to www.weebly.com or www.wix.com These sites will help you build a website and host it for you. If this is your very first time and you're not really sure about things then try it out!

If this is something you KNOW you want to do and you will be making many more websites in the future, get yourself a good Web Host. Make sure you choose the option to host MULTIPLE SITES. Because it's really quick and easy to set up the 2nd, 3rd, 4th sites.

Finally – Redirect your Website name to your Host Server!

STEP 3 Set up the domain and theme in your host

You purchased your domain. Now it's time to set it up. Go to your C-Panel and Add on domain. No Matter who your host is with, you should have a C-Panel.

- Add Domain in C-Panel
- Add Wordpress
- Grab yourself a nice Theme from https://wordpress.org/themes/ .. Something that will tie in nicely with your Niche. Don't stress too much right now about getting it perfect,we can customise it later on. Download and store on your PC as a .zip file.
- Install your Theme

If you have trouble doing the things above, head over to YouTube and search where you are stuck - i.e... "Add a domain in C Panel" There is a plethora of video tutorials on these subjects.

STEP 4   Upload content and customise your site

Information collection - You need to know your Niche... That's why you chose it.
You need to write at least 3 good articles to post on your site. Start with one then you can branch out from there, but for a nice FULL looking site, you will need a few.

Write them all in a word or text document first. Save each article as a separate document.
Add as much USEFUL information as you can, Read a whole bunch of articles so you can get a feel for layouts, and the way a good article is written.

A word of warning, DON'T COPY and PASTE!! This may seem like a really brilliant idea to get content on your site, but Search Engines are smart. If it senses a string of sentences it has already indexed before, guess what???

Your site will be sent all the way down to the bottom of the list, landing you in GOOGLE JAIL!

Read other information out there, and use it as reference material, rephrase into your own words, use "inverted comma snippets" if you like, but be sure to give a litte shout out to who wrote it. *Always give credit where credit is due!*

This will also add credibility to your website. Remember, you don't have to rewrite the book, your just providing customers with useful information, all in one spot –your Site!

- A Main Page Site – Telling your customers about your website, what they can expect, and how it's going to be useful for them to stay and look around.
- Review Page – Here you want to introduce your product, why it's so good, Features and benefits etc.
- You can have a purchase now button at the bottom of your pages, but I prefer a "Purchase Page". Here you can lay out terms and conditions, money back guarantees and assure them they are making the right decision in proceeding with the purchase.
- Add an "About Me" page.
- Set up social networking icons on your page, these days this is a MUST!

STEP 5   Install the tools (secret)

This is the part where you're going to strive above your competition. There are a number of wordpress plugins we are going to use to help us keep track of what's going on, and help us boost our rankings above the rest. Now, this won't happen overnight, but you will see some magic happen.

- Add the plugin – Yeost SEO. This is one of the BEST tools you will use on any and all of your websites. It will HELP you write a fantastic article, and will give you exact points on what to change on your website page or post to get the BEST SEO RANKINGS.
- Add the plugin – Social Media Share.
- Add the plugin – Google Analytics. You have to track your traffic.
- Add the plugin –GetResponse Intergration. This is how we are going to build our e-mail List.
- Submit your sitemap to google.

*Analytics plug in:Set up your domain name in Google Analytics first, then authorise in WP.

Note: You will need a G-mail account if you have not already got one.

STEP 6   Build your site

You should have your site installed. Now we just need to customise.

Swap out the pages in the downloaded theme with your written pages. Make sure you pay close attention to the way Yoast instructs you. All you should have to do is add in your *Keywords* into the snippet and follow their suggested bulletpoints.

Publish your site!

STEP 7   E-mail marketing

You can do this without E-mail Marketing…but why would you?? You want to build your own E-mail list so you have a constant stream of customers to market your product to. This will take a little to set up, and a little cost, but if you're serious about this Affiliate Marketing thing. Then it's a No Brainer!!

- Set Up your Auto-Responder + Manage your E-mail list - If you haven't got your own Auto Responder, I would suggest signing up with GetResponse.

http://www.hotozent.com/getresponse

- Squeeze Page or E-mail Optin Set-up.

http://tryclickfunnelsfor14days.com/

Clickfunnels is an ideal tool for building your websites, opt-in pages and Sales Funnels. Sign up for their 14 day free trial and spend some time getting to know the process of building your own funnels. This is ideal for grabbing E-mail addresses using opt-in pages, and linking through to your website.

If you REALLY want to get into Clickfunnels, and even sign up as an Affiliate, then take the time to go through their FREE "Retire in 100 days" Affiliate bootcamp.

Its well worth the time and effort, and you can learn ALOT.

http://100dayaffiliatebootcamp.com/

There are 2 ways to get someone's email address. An "Opt In Page" will prompt your customer to add in his or her E-mail address before being given access to your site.
This leaves the customer with 2 choices. Either give you their email and proceed, or Go to another site.

If you have done your job right, and got them to you squeeze page, (usually via a free giveaway, E-book or promise to see a video) then they should be excited to swap their info for what you have offered.

The second way is to have a sign up form on your main page, usually a side banner. The GetResponse Plugin will help you put a nice shiny "Sign up Here" widget on your site. This will leave for customers to sign up for themselves. Just remember to remind them constantly to "Sign up to our newsletter on the home page"!

FREE Giveaway to get people into your funnel

A FREE giveaway, as discussed above is a great way to get people to sign up. But where the hell do I get an E-book? Do I have the right to give someone else's product away?

E-book Production - Fiverr - Type in your keyword and add the letters PLR after https://www.iwriter.com - will write an article for you if you pay them. You can find someone to write something for you on Fiverr aswell.

http://www.hotozent.com/fiverr

IDPLR.com is a reference site with literally THOUSANDS of E-books, software and more you can give away. It's FREE to join, however the Once off $99 membership will give you TENS of THOUSANDS of products to choose from.

http://www.hotozent.com/idplr

Create a new FB + twitter account / page - Link from your Main Site.

First thing to do after making your page is to SHARE it with all your friends and family. You will be surprised how many of them will share your hard work out of support!

Now the site is live and up and running..

Write your email follow up sequence and
–sell additional products

This is where E-mail marketing really shines. The great beauty of your Auto-Responder, is the follow up. Those who didn't purchase your product now, have the chance to when you follow up with them later.

If you have set it up right, they should receive their FIRST e-mail, as soon as they signed up. Something along the lines of "Thanks for joining! Here is the E-book I promised you" And a few days later, automatic message will be sent to the tune of "Hey, how did you like that book I sent you?
 If you're into it, here is another product I have been getting into - (Link to your 2nd affiliate product)", and so on.

Just remember, don't keep bombarding your list with offers.Send your customers something useful, or something enjoyable to read.
RELATE to them, as if they were a mate!

TRACK your affiliate sales

If your anything like me, you probably just DO, without thinking it all the way through. One of the biggest Rookie mistakes is to rush ahead, buy some Facebook advertising, and wait to see the result. But I never stop at one thing. I will start several different campaigns, FB Ads, Google Ads, Solo Ads, E-mail links, and then.... I get some traffic and some sales.... but WHERE DID THEY COME FROM?? It's SO VERY IMPORTANT to understand where you spend money, and what results come from that money spent. You really have to track your sales + expenditure.
Here is a FREE Spreadsheet.
http://www.hotozent.com/SimpleSSLand

Carry on your affiliate journey

Pre-register for the Oz Affiliate School!
This is a step by step video course on Building your Online Affiliate Marketing Business.

http://www.hotozent.com/school

It will take you step by step through the above guide, in much more detail, as well as:
- Social Bookmarking tips
- How to Purchase Traffic + Advertise on a budget
- safe-swaps.com (traffic swap) info guide
- Advanced link building – Constant SEO / Niche forums
- Google backend – Webmaster Tools

And LOTS more.

This will be a paid course, however if your among the first 50 to sign up before the course is launched, the entry fee will be waived! Estimated course Version 1 release is currently scheduled for Jan 2018.
Sign up to stay ahead of the pack.

Plenty more information is available NOW at: http://theozaffiliate.com/
I welcome any feedback, and can be contacted at the address below!

Happy Marketing

Matty Mac, The Oz Affiliate
matt@mattymacos.com
https://www.facebook.com/theozaffiliate/

www.ingramcontent.com/pod-product-compliance
Lightning Source LLC
Chambersburg PA
CBHW031522210526
45464CB00007B/3011